FIVE Leadership Development Lessons

Taking the
OUCH
from
Office
Politics

creative energy options
CEO
PUBLISHING

SYLVIA LAFAIR

Disclaimers

Copyright © 2014 Sylvia Lafair, PhD
ISBN 978-0-9883625-5-0

Printed in the United States of America
Published November 2014

creative energy options

CEO
PUBLISHING

45 Country Place Lane
White Haven, PA 18661
570.636.3858
sylvia@ceoptions.com
www.ceoptions.com

i

Dedication

This book is dedicated to all the courageous individuals who heard the call to go through "Total Leadership Connections." You are the pioneers who, once you learned to look at leadership through new eyes and made the commitment to Observe, Understand and Transform outdated behavior patterns you helped to change the culture of your work environment.

Your willingness to say "It will stop with me" and conversely, "It will start with me" has been an inspiration to so many and it is with deep appreciation that I dedicate this book to all of you.

Acknowledgments

What a joy to write this book and have so many stories from all of you I have worked with to show the power of dialogue and honest communication. I do believe that those of us who are willing to look inside ourselves and then take what we learn into our work and home settings are the hope of the future.

I am blessed to have a wonderful team of colleagues who keep the belief in finding the best possible ways to help individuals and teams become the best they can be. To Barry Ginnetti and Frank Walsh, thank you for helping me see from the eyes of strong and competent men. To Nancy Pennebaker and Marylynn Sauro, thank you for always asking the "and what if" questions.

To my team including Fran Heithaus, Gerri Rogan and my right hand, Debbie Woldanski, thank you for always being ready, willing and able to help in any way possible.

And to Herb.....who could ask for a better kindred spirit to make the journey through both the complex and the carefree. Your willingness to challenge me and to protect me makes all the difference. More to come!!!

Table of Contents

Introduction

We talk all the time. The amount of words that fall from our mouths into the ears of others cannot be measured. If words were money we would all be mega rich.

The quality of our words, ah, that is another story.

Leaders who are worth their weight are weighed by how able they are to make their words count.

Here you will learn to make your words the foundation of a successful leadership career. Whether you are climbing the corporate ladder, are in a family firm, a forceful entrepreneur, or a newbie just starting your work life you will be in a winning position once you learn these five vital lessons to take the OUCH from frustrating conversations.

This book is laser focused on core people issues at work. We all grow up with some "NOTS" that become "KNOTS" in the way we communicate. All of us, at one time or another, think we are "not good enough," "not strong enough," and that others are "not like me." These thoughts tie us up and make us tongue-tied. We second guess ourselves.

Master the following lessons for work relationships and take them home. They work equally well in every setting, work, home, community. Once you learn to follow these ground rules you win and everyone around you will win also.

- Ground Rule #1: Telling the truth is NOT spilling your guts
- Ground Rule #2: Work is NOT a rehab facility

- Ground Rule #3: Dialogue is NOT just emotion and repetition
- Ground Rule #4: Outcomes are best if you stay open NOT attached
- Ground Rule #5: You win when you see everything as connected NOT separate

What the world needs now are leaders who have mastered the art and craft of communication and conflict resolution. If you want to be an exemplary leader, turn the page.

Five Leadership Development Lessons:
Taking the Ouch from Office Politics

Chapter 1: Why Can't We All Just Get Along

Knowledge of human relationships no longer belongs only to the psychology crowd. It belongs to all of us. Every leader or emerging leader in today's workplace needs to look below the surface and answer the age old question when someone shoots himself in the foot "Why did he just do what he did?"

We need to know why she just put her foot in her mouth. Why they have "egg" on their faces.

If you are ever to deal with office politics (and that takes place whether you are in a traditional corporation, an entrepreneurial start-up, a family firm, or a non-profit association) you better get a handle on what makes people tick.

FIRST, look inside. That's right. Look at what flips your lid, what sets your blood boiling, what makes you madder than hell. Once you can begin to name the people and situations that get you hopping mad you can decide what to do about them.

NEXT, pay attention to those around you. How do they respond when someone sets their teeth on edge, when they feel torn to shreds, when they feel like a knife was shoved in their back?

Once you have learned to look at the interactions that occur in all human relationships and figured out how to decode the mixed messages that are always at the heart of office politics you become the real leader you have always wanted to be.

That's right!

Learn to see how behavior patterns you learned (and everyone else has also) in your original organization, the family play out at work and you are in the driver's seat.

YOU BECOME THE TRAILBLAZER!

You lead and others will follow. Why? Because we all deeply want to get along. We just were never given the tools and techniques to be more cooperative and collaborative. So, we flounder and blame. It is the way we have learned for centuries.

Let me put it this way: it is NOT just what you think and feel; and it is not just what he/she/they think and feel. It is the interactions that make all the difference.

That is what this book is about.....about the middle space between YOU and WHOEVER! That is where the action is.

Once you learn how we impact each other and what to do about it, the wonders of the world open to you. I promise.

Chapter 2: Damn it, Listen to ME!!!

In our Western culture, we have not spent adequate time learning how to listen effectively and respond appropriately. Our tendency is to "almost" listen and have our answers ready before the other has even completed their first sentence.

While we learned to talk when we were tiny babies, no one really took the time to teach us how to listen, what to listen for and equally important, what to say when it is our turn.

Most of our conversations have been based on "CYA" behavior, starting when we were toddlers.

Yup, we learned to cover our asses as early as the old sing-song chant "Who took the cookies from the cookie jar" and whether we were chewing on the crunchy morsels or nowhere near the cookie jar, the knee jerk response is "NOT ME."

CONVERSATION: The ways we communicate start with conversation. You know, "Hi how are you?" and the answer is most of the time "Fine, thanks." No matter how we are really feeling.

We are polite and skim the surface. In most situations, this is really OK. We just want to smile and nod and keep it light and easy.

DEBATE: Winners and losers are part of the debate world. For many, this is a fun game and it is based on getting the facts right and beating down your opponent by showing how smart you are. This world is prevalent in politics and in the media.

This still skims the surface in point-counterpoint. There is no real way to drill down and get past the obvious when in a debate. It is punch and jab, punch and jam and may the stronger opponent win.

DIALOGUE: This is the essence of collaboration. It is a powerful way to relate and is a vital force waiting to be harnessed. This is a way of communicating with everyone in your life so you learn to find new, creative answers to difficult questions.

In true dialogue you and another, or many others bring together each person's unique point of view back and forth, back and forth, gathering bits of information until you come to a new and more exciting perspective than could have happened individually. It is the essence of the "aha" moment when those in the dialogue think "I never thought of it this way before."

Using dialogue helps to deal with difficult people in a skillful way so that pour professional relationships do not bog you down.

TRUE COMMUNICATION: Once you begin to see the power of dialogue it becomes addictive. You are no longer satisfied with simplistic answers that are meaningless. Now you are on the road of real leadership where you are able to prevent conflicts and produce cooperation.

Quickly you can see when your buttons get pushed you no longer instinctively lash out in fight mode or hold back in flight mode.

You also become adept at seeing how others start the "gotcha game" and how, as a leader you can put a stop to the behavior that causes so much friction and wasted time at work.

Sound good? Let's get to the 5 leadership lessons to help you communicate clearly and calmly and change not just your life, but the lives of everyone who learns from you.

Chapter 3: Deep Dive to Where the Pearls Are

Office politics begin when someone says something nasty or wants to show you how wonderful they are and make you look like a donkey's behind.

Here is a critical question: "What do you do when someone says something that makes you want to go over and choke them? Do you play the one-up-man-ship game? Do you remain silent and merely smirk at them? Do you walk away in a huff?

Most of us can think of the really, really good thing to say later in the day or when falling asleep that night. There is always a moment of "Gosh, I wish I had said that… or that… or that.

Now you can learn to speak up right then and then and do many things at once.

- You can calm the atmosphere.
- You can think on your feet
- You can raise awareness
- You can invite accountability
- You can solve the problem
- You can show empathy

Begin to practice and become more proficient in asking depth questions rather than accepting the first answer given to you.

Learn to ask probing questions without being intrusive. Turn a comment into a question and watch the magic of dialogue change negatives into positives.

Be vigilant by paying attention to the specific way you construct questions to your work colleagues. Stay alert to tonality and body language as you respond, and watch how others use their voices and bodies in response.

Dialogue is not one question, one answer, out and over. It is more like a stream that eventually runs into the ocean. One question sparks another thought and then another question and another thought. You know when it has come to completion because there is a sense of relaxation and good will among the participants.

Here are some tips to consider: choose from "what, where, when, how, why" when you start your question. Make sure it cannot be answered "yes" or "no" since that stops the river of words from flowing.

Give this method a shot. You will be pleasantly surprised to find responses that have more meat to them.

In this way there are fewer tendencies to become battle ready and defend a position.

YOU can start new ways of communicating and stop the office politics from spreading like a virus through the office.

Next let's look at empathic listening and how as a leader you can use this tool to become a hero at work.

Ground Rule #1:

Telling the Truth is

NOT

Spilling Your Guts!

Chapter 4: Tell the Truth! It's a Powerful Method for Leading Effectively

I will begin with a story from one of the teams I consulted with and an emerging leader who almost went down in flames.

I have been teaching the art form of telling the truth as one of the most important aspects of leadership that lasts over time.

Andrea was a great student and paid attention to everything I suggested. However, as is often the case, too much of anything can become toxic. And that was Andrea's initial issue.

Imagine you were with us at a seaside resort for a three day off-site to plan for the New Year. There were 18 people on her sales team, a gung-ho group that was ready to knock it out of the park and be first in the company in sales.

Day one of the off-site was high energy and lots of new ideas came forward. The team had learned to use empathic listening and ask open-ended questions and walk down the spiral road of dialogue to find new solutions to old problems.

Day two looked like it was also headed for a home run. That is until…

Dan, one of the top guns in sales started to challenge his boss Andrea. Suddenly everything I had been teaching about listening and responding and dialogue fell to the wayside and it became the old model of defend, explain, and justify.

Dan was a really bright guy and he had a war chest full of "gotchas" that he was flinging at everyone in the group. I waited to see how Andrea, as the leader would respond to his nastiness.

She sat like a deer in the headlights and I began to squirm in my chair getting ready to take charge. As a consultant I was frustrated, hoping they had all learned enough to get past this roadblock.

It was not happening. You see, when stress hits the hot button we all tend to revert to ingrained, outdated behavior patterns to stay safe. It doesn't' work and only adds more fuel to the fire. However, it takes lots of practice to stay in dialogue and not get swayed by office politics.

I finally got Andrea's attention and was ready for her to show all the great stuff she had learned by being in our Total leadership Connections Program.

Nope! She too reverted to her pattern of finger-pointing and blame. The "dialogue" ended up a debate and it was ugly.

"Dan", she took control. "Dan, you are out of line. While you are a top notch sales person your behavior on the team is disgusting."

That got everyone's attention.

Dan sat up straight in his chair and glowered at Andrea.

He shot back, "You have no right to talk with me like that. What kind of a leader are you to call me disgusting?"

"I am talking about your behavior" Andrea said with an "I dare you to keep talking" look on her face.

Andrea then took telling the truth to a whole new level of upset. Was she telling her truth? Yes. Was it going to forward the action? No.

Before Dan could say anything else Andrea launched into all of her frustrations with this man in front of the whole team. "You are cracker- jack at sales yet, have you ever noticed that the rest of the team never asks you for advice? It is because you are so stuck on yourself and all you do is brag, brag, and brag."

With that I had to jump in and stop the bloodshed.

We took a break and I took Andrea into a private room and said to her in wonder, "What were you thinking?"

Her response led me to change the first of the 5 leadership lessons to get even clearer.

"You said that it is important for leaders to tell the truth and that is what I did."

I sighed in exasperation, "Andrea let me change this and NEVER forget what I am about to say:

"Telling the truth is NOT spilling your guts."

We went back to a very shattered team. The thinking was "if she can do that to Dan, am I next?"

It took months for Andrea to repair the damage at the off-site. Hard way to learn, yet learn she did.

What did she have to do to make her team function in a healthy manner again? The next chapter gives you the clues.

Chapter 5: Do It Differently

Andrea learned, once again, that the key question in back of a leader's mind must be "How can what I am about to say forward the situation and make a positive difference."

When you tell the truth, especially when you are angry or disappointed, remember you are not meant to spill your guts or setup a situation where you gather votes to prove you are right.

You know you are going into deep doo-doo when you say "and furthermore, Robert and Sarah agree with me." My observation of truth telling is that sentences are short; they do not run on and on into rambling paragraphs.

Truth sentences are around seven to twelve words. And when you finish the sentence you need to sop and breathe and maintain some moments of quiet before anyone begins to speak.

Here is what Andrea learned from the altercation with Dan.

Here is what a leader will do to take the ping out of the pain and not let the office politics gather steam.

"Dan, I want to thank you for your comments. And I would like to know what your intention is from what you just said." Then Andrea could have taken a deep breath and waited for Dan to respond.

Think about it for a minute. Andrea in this scenario does not attack nor blame. She simply asks him to be accountable for his actions.

What will Dan respond? It all depends on how safe it is in the room. It all depends upon Dan's level of understanding himself. Regardless of how Dan responds, Andrea is still very much in a power position as a leader. No one is sitting there thinking that she may want to take them out next. In fact, there is relief that she is asking Dan to respond in a grown-up and responsible manner.

Further leadership training: if Dan stays on his arrogant position it would be beneficial for Andrea to meet with him privately or have a coach or H.R. representative talk with him about how his behavior is impacting the team.

This leads to leadership lesson #2 that can save a lot of time and grief once it is understood.

Ground Rule #2:

Work Is NOT A Rehab Facility!

Chapter 6: How to Help Without Being Trapped

Most leaders in the 21st Century want to help their direct reports succeed. The world of work is less like the days of bosses telling and employees simply doing what they are told without question.

Often, as you, the leader become more aware of the behavior patterns that keep people from doing their best work that more time than is healthy is spent in the process of "helping."

Remember, either end of the pendulum will create work havoc.

We know that hidden patterns of behavior can wreak havoc in the workplace. They rear their ugly heads in the form of power games, snide comments, unfinished work, and a variety of disruptive behavior. Harboring old and often hurtful memories, we react to problems with preconceived notions about how our reactions with bosses, peers, and direct reports will turn out. And these mind games usually become self-fulfilling prophecies.

If not tacked and changed a circle of predictability ensues that produces ineffective behavior, poor work performance, misused sick days and the worst of office politics, gossip and rumor mongering.

Advanced emotional and social intelligence requires a strong comprehension of the working of the world of the interactive world of relationships and systems thinking.

Back to the idea of leaders as mentors and helpers.

Unless you are a coach, or H.R. specialist who is destined to work with the deeper aspects of workplace behavior the rule of three is the one to follow.

First, all the research indicates that for a behavior pattern to change it takes approximately three months. So, please do not expect a change to occur and stick from the very first time you say something to help one of your direct reports or peers.

If by the third time in three months you have to go over the same retread territory and there is no viable change it is time to take action with a different type of intervention.

Your part is to be committed to continued truth telling and active listening. You need to be involved if the employee is remaining with the company. This means being kept in the loop as to how the coaching is proceeding. However, the work now belongs to the coach or to HR.

If there is no willingness to make change happen then, once you are clear that you have given the situation a fair reading you must, and that is must, make decisions for the betterment of the team and the organization.

Nothing is as demoralizing as watching someone who is not a team player and who is not fielding their share of the work stay and, in effect, smirk at the leader and the organization unwilling to take a stand.

While you, as a leader, need to be in tune with your emotions, you need not be driven by them.

Nest chapter is about what to listen for in a meeting, in a small group, one-one.

Ground Rule #3:

Dialogue is

NOT

Just Emotion and Repetition!

Chapter 7: Saying the Same Things Over and Over, Only Differently

One of my coaching clients was telling me about the new CTO who was brought on to his company as a surprise. He is basically an uninvited entrant into the company.

We all figured he was a relative or he was sleeping his way to the top. Not nice, but honest.

"We were already upside down when the CEO retired and the new gal came in. Just as we got used to the newness of the situation and decided she was pretty savvy and we could live with the situation and with her they announced the new CTO. This guy has no real bearing on our type of technology. We all thought our boss would get the job. He has been with the company for a long time and is well-respected. It was like a swift kick to the gut.

Everyone has their heads down and is playing it safe. And by playing it safe, I mean we all have our resumes on the street. I still cannot understand how dumb an organization can be to come from behind with such a poor choice.

We are all getting stress related stuff and many are out with sore throats and viruses and it is not even cold season."

First, check what is going on at work by checking your own physical responses. If you feel queasy, uneasy or conflicted, pay attention. If you feel like you've been kicked in the gut or your heart begins to race, pay attention.

Dealing with office politics means understanding that emotions can run rampant at work. We do pick up each other's anxieties.

Did you ever hear of mirror neurons? That is part of what is going on here.

All the research in neuropsychology has been amazing in helping us understand much of what goes on at work (and in our personal relationships too).

Let's dig a bit deeper. Mirror neurons are a type of brain cell that respond equally when we perform an action as well as when we see someone else performing the same action. This concept seems simple yet, implications are far reaching.

It's like watching a movie of someone being hurt and we automatically cringe, even though we are sitting quietly in a room with no disturbance. Or when someone shows a great deal of empathy toward another and we well up with positive emotion.

The neural mechanism is involuntary and automatic. We don't have to think about what other people are doing or feeling, we simply know. It seems we are wired to see other people are similar to ourselves rather than different.

Thus in the work situation where the new CTO came in unexpectedly he was viewed as "enemy" and those who worked together began to feel similar emotions.

It is vital that leaders not be caught up in "sheep mentality" and continually ask yourself what you are experiencing as discussions develop. This takes some discipline to stay at observation of what is going on and not get caught up in the emotional wave of the moment.

When you listen it is important to think about key phrases that are repeated over and over. You may hear "We are not being included" or "They think we cannot make good decisions" or "it was his fault or her fault or their fault and I am not to blame."

Phrases or words that are repeated over and over have a strong "feeling tone" to them and that is the time for leaders to decipher what is going on with accountability questions as discussed earlier.

Just to refresh your memory. Accountability questions are:

"What do you want as an outcome from this discussion?" Or "What is your intention in bringing this up right now?" Or "How do you plan to solve this problem and who do you need to help with it?"

When you, as a leader do not get caught up in the emotional turmoil yet are able to acknowledge it you are in a strong position to help your team and company move forward without all the bitterness and back-biting that often accompanies change.

Ground Rule #4:

Outcomes are Best if You Stay Open

NOT

Attached!

Chapter 8: Stay Open to Change your Mind

Think about this for a moment. You would not wear the same clothes for weeks at a time. Nor would you only eat hamburgers or tofu burgers for months on end. So what the heck is wrong with changing your mind?

We get concerned and riled up when someone says "let's change direction." And you hear those behind closed door voices saying "But, BUT, she was always so consistent. And now, we have no leader and no direction.'

Hey, life happens. What leaders need more than ever is flexibility and the ability to make new decisions based on the most up to date information available.

Now, I don't mean change just for the sake of change. I mean check out the assumptions and know that the only constant in life is to change when it is necessary.

You know the old saying

"If you always do what you have always done,
You will always get what you have always gotten."

Habits and patterns are comfortable because we know what to expect. However, that is not called progress. It is called playing it safe.

Being clear and decisive does not in any way keep you from changing your perspective and following a new direction.

Now as you learn to use open ended questions in your quest for clarity know the direction you want to go. Before you open the dialogue ask yourself:

21

- Is this a fact finding dialogue
- Is this a time to learn more about the other person
- Is this a time to reassess how you work together
- Is this a time to create a performance improvement plan
- Is this a time to decide to add more people to the team

The more you think through what you want as an outcome the more it becomes possible for you to get what you want.

Know that there are personal patterns that it is up to YOU to transform. There are also organizational patterns that keep progress from being made.

Organizational patterns that need to be changed are those that have judgment, blame, or attack at the core. This model has been a basic one for eons and stifles creative conversations.

When you feel yourself starting the blame game or becoming too judgmental take a moment STOP, BREATHE, and then begin again.

Dialogue will give room for you to continue in a more user friendly way where you and the other person can let new, useful ideas into the room.

If you really want to become an expert in understanding patterns and how they stop the free flowing energy of the workplace watch a few films that show how people get trapped in old paradigms. "The Wolf of Wall Street" is a great example of how mirror neurons take over and how the need to be a super achiever measured by money creates an ugly mess.

Other films to check out about patterns at work are: "Nine to Five", "The Matrix", and "Wall Street".

Ground Rule #5:

You Win When You See Everything as Connected

NOT

Separate!

Chapter 9: Independent? Nah, that's the Biggest Myth Going!

You know the old cowboy films with the strong silent guy who did what he did without needing anyone in his life?

That myth of the Clint Eastwood type of dude led to lots of disappointments when it comes to real relationships.

First off, we are all, yes all, born from a relationship (that sperm and that egg belong to two different people) then we come through a relationship (mom and baby work at it together) and then we come into this world into a relationship (be it parent, parents, caregiver).

No one survives alone. NO ONE!

Now let's bring this thinking about how things are connected into the workplace.

Want the same old, same old? Then don't stretch your mind. Want transformation? Then stay with me right now and pay attention.

The true key to transformation is to look at life holistically and think about how the parts of a system connect rather than merely look at superficial problems.

Just about every company I work with still has frustrations about the silo mentality. Ah, the silo mentality. My part of the organization is the main driver and what we need is the most important.

Being in a silo sets up nonporous boundaries and limits cooperation between the various parts of an organization. This creates patterned, rigid roles being played out without thinking through either the short term or especially the long term implications.

And guess where office politics comes from? That's right, from outdated patterns of "mine is more important that yours" and "I need and you don't" and 'we will win at all costs and who really cares if you lose.'

This game is interactive and can be deadly. So long as we do not take the time and use our intelligence to observe how marketing and sales and procurement and research and development are connected we lose and the organization loses.

When teams begin to think systemically wonders happen.

Take the sales and marketing group that had come together for a meeting. Each individual was asked to take a few minutes and say where they see their successes and where they need help. By the time the group was finished it was clear that the marketing team had some super ideas to put into play but money had run out for new projects in this, the third quarter.

After a snack break the head of sales said she would like to speak.

"At the break we decided that since we are one company and that 'we are all in it together' we would like to gift the marketing team with the money they need to fund the new project. We know this kind of thing is not ever really done, however, if we are going to change the company culture to one that is more interconnected and productive, why not let it start with us?"

This was one of those 'you have got to be kidding' moments that quickly turned into a meaningful discussion of the essence of real change and how to sustain it.

Fast forward six months.

The company had begun to change at a core level. The silo mentality was melting fast and people across both

26

corporate and around the country were relying on each other in new and positive ways.

Another amazing bonus for all the goodwill created by people helping, came in the form of a traditional bonus. At the end of the year the teams were gifted with lots of extra cash to share with their families. The lesson learned is if one of us wins, we all win. And that is an idea worth sharing.

Chapter 10: Leadership Lessons

You have the 5 leadership lessons and now you are ready for a list of guidelines to keep in mind as you continue to grow and add to your leadership backpack of tips and techniques. Copy this list and keep it somewhere close so you can do a review every so often. This list is what we call "evergreen" and will never go out of season.

Remember:
- Dialogue trumps debate and casual conversation when it comes to effecting real and lasting change.
- Be ultra-observant of what you say and how you use words so that you do not get caught in pattern repetition.
- Become more conscious of what your gut has to tell you and trust your intuition.
- Create pattern interrupt situations such as changing when you speak in a meeting by going first if you always go last and vice versa.
- Practice truth sentences that are short and do not include blame or attack.
- Probe beyond the obvious by using open ended questions that start with 'how' 'what' 'when' and 'why.'
- Keep a journal that you write in at the end of the day to track where you were 'pattern aware' and where you got trapped in your old behaviors.
- Get an accountability buddy who you talk with once a week and remember this is not about spilling your guts, it is about not falling back into old behaviors.

- Keep a visual touchstone on your desk or the words from a quote or song that will help you stay steady when your old patterns start to push forward.
- Tell the important parts of your story that can give hope to others as you lead them into new and positive territory to become the best they can be at work.

As a leader you are taking the role of change agent. You do not have to be on the 'bleeding edge' of change, where you are so far ahead of others that they think you are speaking a foreign language. However, to lead with power you need to be on the leading edge and be willing to take risks to make the changes helpful and long lasting.

The process of change has certain basic components that must be considered: there is anxiety and stress, and a subtle yet potent demand to maintain the status quo. At the same time there is an underlying yearning for change and growth.

It is this tension that you as a leader need to harness and lead your team through the desire to keep things the way they have been out of fear of the new.

There is what I like to call "the ugly middle" of the process of change that every leader must contend with:

- Gossip will increase and change is demanded
- Paranoia increases and people become fearful that they will lose their jobs
- People take sides and need to prove that their way is the better way
- Cliques develop
- People feel overworked and under valued
- There is an increase in stress related illnesses and absenteeism increases

- People want quick solutions and want to be told what to do
- The 'gotcha game' activates to unpleasant levels

During this difficult time of change it is up to you to stay on course and not be made to feel guilty that you are leading the direction for change. It is important that you not get caught in "JUBLA" where you Judge, blame or attack. It is a time to say "I hear you" when the complaining occurs and not give long winded explanations. It is a time to say "This is where we are going and I need you to join me."

Once you, as a leader begin the process of listening and using the power of dialogue with your team and own the fact that you are helping to shape the new way at work you start to develop a strong presence.

There are no words to describe presence. It is like truth or trust, you know it when you see it. With presence you become authentic and there is no better place to be in your life, personally and professionally.

Sylvia Lafair, PhD has dedicated her career to helping individuals become their best. First as a psychologist working with families and couples and then making a left hand turn into the world of business leadership and team development.

Her "UNIQUE" ideas have had widespread influence in corporations, family firms, and entrepreneurial start-ups.

The past 25 years have been spent helping executives, managers, and teams connect the dots of how personal and professional behavior cannot be separated. She has trained a staff of executive coaches and facilitators in her Pattern Aware™ model.

What has been eye-opening in all manner of organizations is that when stress hits the hot button we all tend to revert to patterns from childhood that were there to keep us safe. While they may have helped at five or seven or twelve, they can run havoc in adult relationships.

Working with companies around the world it became clear that the universal aspects of what it means to be in relationships is not very different regardless of culture, size of company, or product. Everywhere there is the yearning for all of us to get along. Dr. Lafair's innovative work gives us the directives to make this happen.

Her book *'Don't Bring It to Work'* has won nine awards and with its companion *'Pattern Aware Success Guide,'* has been used in graduate programs and by work teams worldwide.

Her book, *'GUTSY: How Women Leaders Make Change'* has also won six book awards and led to her highly successful **GUTSY Women Weekend Retreats**.

This newest book *'UNIQUE: How Story Sparks Diversity, Inclusion and Engagement,'* is based on the powerful model of storytelling called **Sankofa Mapping ™**.

Dr. Lafair's abilities to blend story with fact and humor make her a sought after speaker, workshop facilitator, and executive coach.

Her **Total Leadership Connections Program ™**, now in its fourteenth year, has been named one of the top leadership development programs in 2014 by Leadership Excellence/H.R.com, making this the third year in a row.

Dr. Lafair has been featured in *The Wall Street Journal, Forbes* and *Time* as well as on the *Today Show* with Kathie Lee and Hoda.

For further information or to book Dr. Lafair for a consultation or speaking engagement please call her office at 570.636.3858 or email her directly at sylvia@ceoptions.com.

9 780988 362550